THE GOLF DRILLS, DISTILLED

Illustrated Guide to the Best Golf Drills

PETE STYLES

The publisher Golf Distillery Inc. and the author Pete Styles cannot be held responsible for any injuries, which may occur as a result of these golf exercises. The publisher and author also disclaim any liability of any kind for losses or damages caused or alleged to be caused directly, or indirectly, from using the information contained herein.

Published by
Golf Distillery - Extracting the Essence of Golf

Ebook ISBN: 978-1-7381706-2-3
Paperback ISBN: 978-1-7381706-3-0
Hardcover ISBN: 978-1-7381706-4-7

Golf Distillery

TABLE OF CONTENTS

INTRODUCTION

to the "Golf, Distilled" Series

I have a passionate belief that anyone can play consistently great golf. That belief comes from delivering thousands of lessons to players from every walk of life and at every level.

What I've found is that when you commit just a short amount of time to really ingraining the proven fundamentals of golf, it transforms your game.

Fundamentals might not be new. They might not seem exciting either – especially when you read about "magic moves" and "undiscovered swing secrets" in glossy magazines and elsewhere on the internet.

But mastering the fundamentals is exciting. Very exciting. Why? Because it delivers.

It gives you everything you want from the game – solid, crisp ball striking, booming drives that split the fairway in two, penetrating irons, masterful touch and feel and of course... consistency – in every area of your game.

I'm sure you already know that golfers can spend years chasing one gimmick after another without seeing any long-term improvement in their game. The irony is that if they just spent a fraction of that time mastering the key fundamentals of golf, they'd have a great swing... a swing for life.

That's the aim of this series of illustrated guides: to inspire you to become the great golfer you can be... and to give you step-by-step lessons to help achieve it!

Pete Styles, PGA Class A Professional
Over 75 000 lessons delivered
Manchester, England, UK

THE GOLF DRILLS, DISTILLED

1 - TAKEAWAY DRILLS

1.1 KEEP THE CLUBFACE IN FRONT OF YOUR CHEST

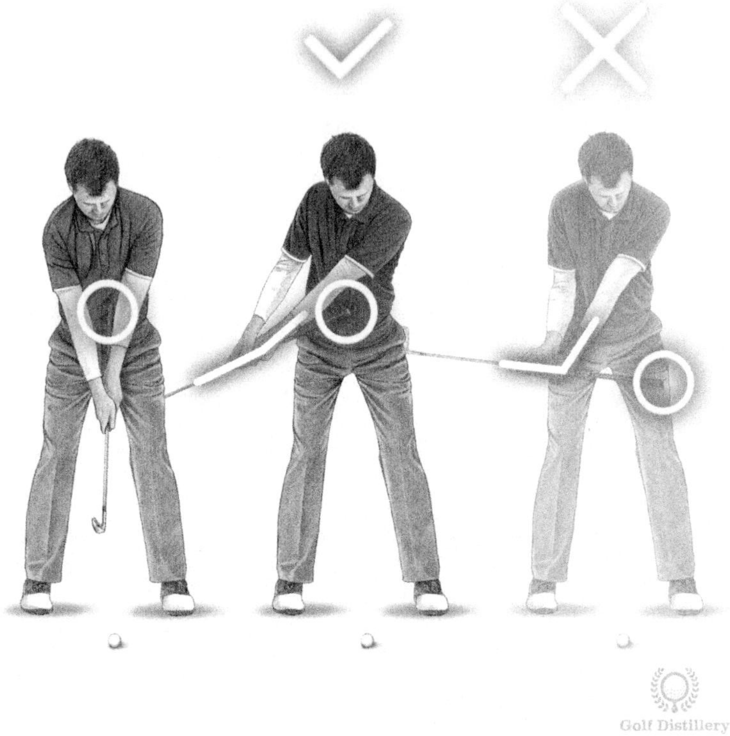

Here's a great little drill if you're struggling to get the feeling of a one-piece takeaway in your golf swing.

It will help you to co-ordinate the initial movement of your hands, arms, midsection and chest – so that they all move in unison on a good path during the initial take-away phase.

- Take your normal setup, then slide your hands down the club shaft until the butt end of the club rests into your belly button.

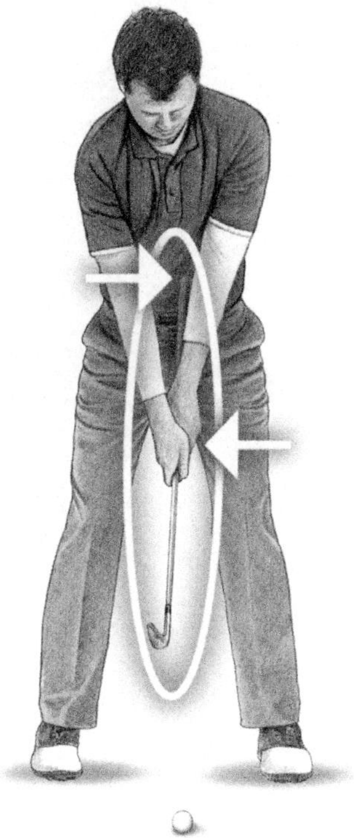

- Now start your backswing, turning your left shoulder under your chin. Make sure your hands are passive (no wrist hinge or rotation) so that you create a 'one-piece' takeaway.

- The butt end of the club should stay fixed into your stomach until the clubhead reaches about hip height. If you are using too much hand or arm action during this phase, you will notice that the club becomes detached from your belly button.

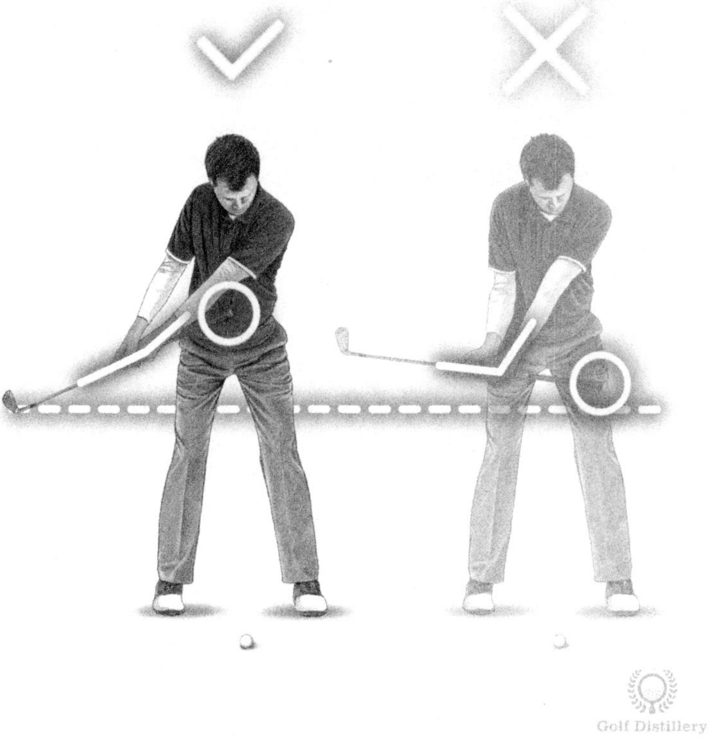

1.2 KEEP YOUR HANDS FROM ROLLING OVER

Here's another very simple but very useful golf drill to help you with the one-piece takeaway.

I use a range basket but you could just as easily use a basketball or beach ball.

- Holding a range basket, take your normal setup over the ball.

- Go ahead and make a one-piece turn until the basket is about hip height.

- There should be no twisting or rotating of the basket as you take it away. If you were to look in a mirror facing down-the-line of your target, you'd be able to see right inside the basket.

2 - BACKSWING DRILLS

2.1 BRING THE CLUB UP ON THE CORRECT PATH

This excellent backswing drill is simple but very informative. It will help you get a feel for your swing path and whether you're swinging the club on too-flat or too-steep a plane.

• Find an area where you can use a wall to check the path of your backswing. Take your setup so that your backside just touches the wall as you set up to the ball. You may want to grip the club at the opposite end (near the clubhead) to avoid damaging your club or the wall.

- Take the club away until the clubhead is roughly hip height. Ensure that the club is parallel to the wall and parallel to the ground at this level. This will help you spot an inside or outside takeaway position.

- Continue to the halfway back position. The club should touch the wall **at or around head height.**

- If it touches the wall at hip, chest or shoulder height, you are taking the club back too much on an **inside path**.

- If the club doesn't touch the wall at all or way above head height, you are taking the club back too much on the **outside**.

Side note: I used a 7-iron to demonstrate this backswing drill. You can try it with different clubs but be aware that because your posture is changing along with the length of the club, the clubhead should come into contact with the wall at different heights. For example, a driver should touch the wall lower down – at about shoulder height. A pitching wedge should touch the wall way above head height, if at all.

2.2 POSITION OF THE CLUB DURING THE BACKSWING

This backswing drill will help you to set the club in a nice position halfway back.

One of my favourite checkpoints for good swing path and swing plane involves the position of the hands at the midway point – they should appear directly in front of your chest if you were to look in a mirror facing down-the-line behind you.

This backswing drill will help you get into that good checkpoint position more easily and more consistently.

- Place the left hand on the club in the normal position and place the right hand further down – around 5 inches below the base of the grip. Allow the club to stay around 18 inches off the ground.

- As you turn your shoulders, allow the left arm to stay straight and the right arm to bend to 90 degrees. Only swing the club to chest height and check that the butt end of the grip points at the ball.

- If you have a mirror available, use a down-the-line view to check that the right hand is positioned directly in the centre of your chest.

3 -TOP OF THE SWING DRILLS

3.1 HOW TO ROTATE YOUR UPPER BODY CORRECTLY

This simple drill will show you if your shoulders are turning correctly through to the completion of the backswing. A nice, full shoulder turn will help you to generate power. What this drill can also highlight is the action of your legs.

Golfers that lack flexibility, particularly in their lower and upper backs, struggle to turn their shoulders to 90-degrees. To compensate (so they can still feel like they're getting a full turn), they allow too much hip turn and/or a lot of knee action.

But as you'll see, a lot of hip rotation and knee action during the backswing results in a huge loss of power and tremendous instability for the downswing.

Try the following drill and if you find that either your shoulders aren't turning close to 90 degrees, or they are but with the help of a lot of hip turn and leg action, consider trying to improve your flexibility.

- Take your normal setup and then place a club across your shoulders so that the butt end of the club points towards your intended target.

• Now start to make your normal backswing. Feel your shoulders reach a 90 degree turn. This now points the butt end of the club towards the ball.

- Your hips should turn by less than 20 degrees and your legs should remain stable. A weight shift should take place allowing for 60 percent of your bodyweight to move in to the instep of your right foot. Too much leg action will cause instability and a poor weight transfer.

3.2 WHERE TO POSITION THE CLUB AT THE TOP

This second drill is more of a checkpoint to help you to assess your swing plane and path during the backswing. It's a great way to make sure you're not swinging the club on too-flat or too-steep a plane.

If you're in too-flat or too-steep a position at the top, you'll have to work hard during the downswing to deliver the club correctly into the ball. You'll find it difficult to achieve any real consistency.

On the other hand, a good position at the top gives you a much greater chance of producing a good downswing – which allows you to strike the ball solidly and towards your intended target.

- Take a normal backswing and hold the position at the top.

- From this top position, allow the club to drop and notice where it lands. If it lands towards the edge of your shoulder bone, that tells you that you're swinging the club on a nice plane and path up to the top of the backswing.

- If the club misses your shoulder all together as you let it drop, that tells you that you're swinging the club on too-flat a plane – too much around your body. The position of the club at the top is in what we call a 'laid-off' position.

- If the club hits you towards the top of your right shoulder – near your neck – you are swinging the club on too-steep a path.

3.3 WHERE TO POINT THE CLUB AT THE TOP

This drill will help you to achieve the correct position at the top of the backswing by focusing on your left thumb.

You may have heard golf coaches and players talk about being 'across the line' in golf.

This simply means that, for the right-handed golfer, the club is pointing to the right of the target at the top of the backswing (assuming you're looking down-the-line, in the position the camera would be).

Ideally, we want the club to point straight down-the-line at your intended target at the top (see previous illustration). From this position, it will be much easier to consistently control the path of your downswing and hence the accuracy of your shots.

Because you can't see the club at the top, it's difficult to know exactly where it's pointing. A good way to gauge this is to focus on your left thumb.

3.4 HOW TO POSITION THE RIGHT HAND AT THE TOP

For the right-handed golfer, you'll see a lot written and talked about the position of the left hand – particularly at the top of the backswing.

But for this drill, I'd like you to consider the position of your right hand at the top of the backswing.

Focusing on your right hand helps you to get the club in an ideal position at the top (not too flat, or what we call 'laid-off', and not too steep).

This in turn will allow your downswing to travel on the most efficient path into the ball – with the net result being a better ball strike and more consistent golf.

It's also quite easy for most right-handed golfers to focus on, and alter, their right hand position (and vice versa for left handers), so you should find this checkpoint easy to work with.

- At the top of the backswing, the right elbow should be bent at around 90 degrees.

- The right wrist should also be bent at about 90 degrees so that the palm of the right hand faces directly at the sky (back of the hand is parallel to the ground).

- Your right elbow should be below the right shoulder.

- A good image is to think about how waiters would carry a tray of drinks.

4 - DOWNSWING DRILL

4.1 PROMOTE GOOD WEIGHT TRANSFER

This downswing drill will help you with the transitional part of your golf swing.

The transition is one of the most important parts of your swing – it's that changing from the top of the backswing to the start of the downswing.

There are a couple of key movements in the downswing and the first is driving your bodyweight off the right side and onto the left side (for the right-handed golfer).

A mistake I see in a lot of amateur golfers is a downswing that begins too much with the hands and arms pulling the club into the ball. Instead, we need to begin the downswing with a drive of the hips to transfer weight correctly.

One of the ways you can do this is to think about your right heel at the top of the backswing. We want the right heel to lift before we get to impact.

The heel normally lifts as a result of the hips driving across, but you can try exaggerating that movement of the heel to get a feel for an early drive and a bit of extra weight transfer.

- From the top of your backswing, feel as though your right heel pushes off the ground to drive your bodyweight over to the left.

4.2 KEEP THE LAG AS YOU BRING THE CLUB DOWN

This quick and simple downswing drill will help you to bring the club down into the ball on the right path.

Golfers that slice the ball tend to bring the club down on an out-to-in swing path, cutting across the golf ball. Likewise, hook shots are often caused by a swing path that is too flat and on too much of an in-to-out swing path.

A nice way to get the club travelling down on plane (not too steep and not too flat) is to place a tee peg in the top of the grip to act as a visual marker.

- Place a long tee peg in the hole at the end of the grip.

- Pause at the top of your backswing and pull the club down by focusing on pulling the tee peg into the back of the ball.

- Also, as the club reaches a position that is parallel to the ground, make sure that the tee peg is pointing directly down your target line.

4.3 PROTECT YOURSELF FROM *OVER THE TOP*

This simple downswing drill will help to ensure your downswing is on a good path and plane.

A lot of amateur golfers (perhaps even the majority) would benefit from a more in-to-out swing path. This drill helps to promote that by having you focus on one specific area of your body – your right elbow (left elbow for left-handed players).

It's a simple drill but give it a try at the range – particularly if you find yourself hitting pulls or slices.

- Split the hands so that the left hand is placed normally on the club. Place the right hand 5 inches below the grip.

- Take your swing to the top and then pause as you feel how the right elbow should start the downswing with a vertical drop towards your right hip pocket.

- Try to avoid letting your right elbow move too far forwards in front of your body at this stage.

5 - IMPACT DRILLS

5.1 IMPROVE YOUR BALL STRIKING

One of the key positions that you can try and help yourself get into at impact is a strong left side (for the right-handed golfer).

You'll often hear a lot of better players talk about hitting against a firm left side – it helps them to generate more power and greater stability through impact.

Important side note: if you have knee problems or a weak left side (hip, ankle, etc.) you might need a little bit of knee bend to soften the action and reduce any strain on a problem area.

Professional golfers can struggle with injury because of a very aggressive, almost snapping-like, movement with the left knee at impact. But remember, they've been hitting hundreds of golf balls every day at speeds and forces that most of us don't come close to.

- Use a mirror to view your swing from head on. This will help you to check that as you bring the club down towards impact, the left leg straightens or snaps backwards just before impact.

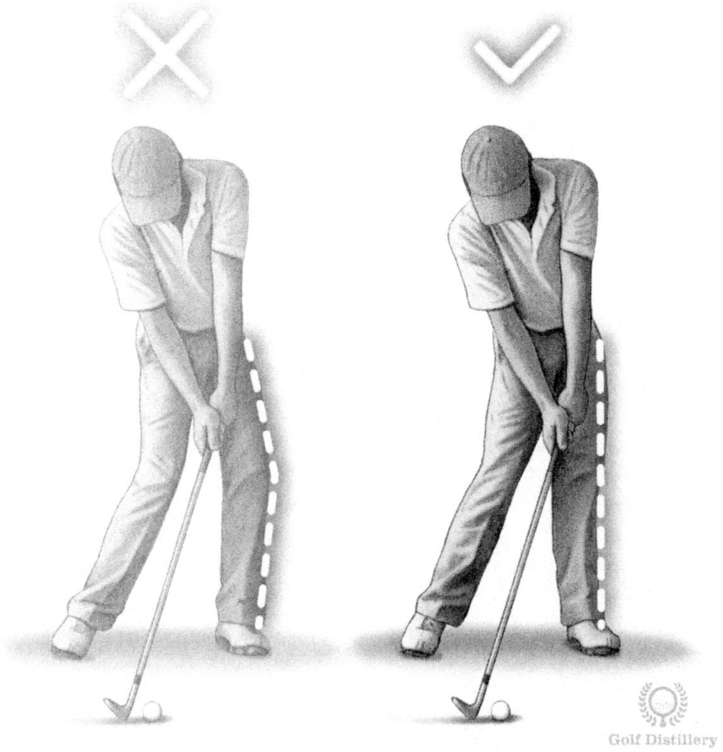

- The feeling that you are trying to create is that you are hitting into a solid, straight left side that will support the bodyweight as it shifts aggressively onto it.

A reminder that if you have knee problems you should avoid aggressively snapping you knee into a locked position.

5.2 STRENGTHEN YOUR IMPACT POSITION

These two impact drills will help you to feel the sensations of a solid impact position.

If you're familiar with the impact position checkpoints you'll appreciate what a good position at impact consists of – but it's not always easy to recreate those checkpoints when you're swinging the club at speed.

Using an impact bag or performing the static press drill are great alternatives.

As you'll see from the static press drill, you don't need an impact bag – you can simply use the bottom of your golf bag out on the range or even as part of a pre-round warm-up.

During the winter months, you can try the static press drill at home using a door frame to press the club against. It will help you to maintain that feeling of a solid impact position even when you're unable to hit balls.

– IMPACT BAG

- Address the bag as you'd address the ball, in a good setup position.
- Make a couple of very easy swings, striking the bag using about 25% effort.
- Gradually work up to a maximum of 75% effort, noticing and feeling the position of your body at impact each time.

- Feel how your body reacts – your hands should stay forwards, your bodyweight should drive to the front foot, the hips and shoulders will turn and open up but your head and chest should stay down.

– STATIC PRESS

- For this drill, you'll need something solid that will provide a level of resistance. As you can see from the drawing you can just use the base of your golf bag.
- Set the club at the base of the golf bag in a good address position. Instead of making a backswing, just apply some forward pressure to the club. Try to drive the bag along the ground.

- While doing so, again feel how your body reacts – your hands should stay forwards, your bodyweight should drive to the front foot, the hips and shoulders will turn and open up but your head and chest should stay down.
- Hold each press for 5 seconds and relax. Repeat 5-10 times before hitting some balls (starting with a shorter iron) trying to repeat the same sensations at impact.

6 - RELEASE AND EXTENSION DRILLS

6.1 PROPER ARM ROTATION

This drill will help you with correct arm rotation through the golf ball.

Extending and rotating correctly through the golf ball is something that a lot of club players struggle with. It costs them both power and accuracy. In fact, learning to rotate your arms and hands fully is a great way to generate extra power and distance without any extra exertion in the swing.

- Take your grip on the golf club as normal but then slide your bottom hand (right hand for the right-handed golfer) down the club so it's gripping the club shaft one hand's width below the bottom of the grip.

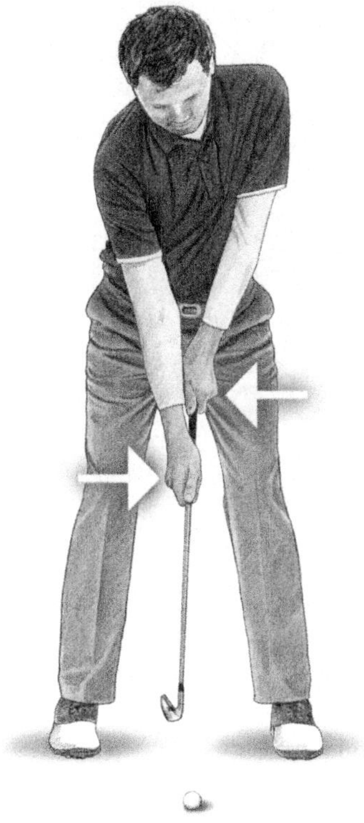

- Make a shortened backswing making sure the left arm stays straight and then swing through to a follow through position and hold. In that completed position both arms should be straight and fully extended.

- You will notice a very aggressive crossover or rotation of the hands during the swing. The rotation is exaggerated in this drill because the right hand (which is gripping right down the shaft) has to travel much further, and so much faster, than the left hand.

- Make half a dozen swings with your hands split like this and then slide your bottom hand up a few inches. Make some more swings replicating that rotational feeling. Repeat the process, each time sliding your right hand up the club until you are taking a normal grip.

6.2 PROPER HAND ROTATION

Here's another drill to help you achieve correct arm and hand rotation through the golf ball.

- Grip the club as normal (a mid-iron is a good club to begin with) but hold it out in front of you so that it's horizontal to the ground.

- Make a baseball-type backswing and make some full swings around your body – all the while keeping the club parallel to the ground.

- As the club reaches a point directly in front of your chest, stop your swing and notice at what angle the clubhead is pointing. We want the toe of the club to point directly up at the sky.

- Notice how, from the backswing to the follow through, your right and left hands swap positions (in the backswing your left hand is on top, in the follow through your right hand is on top).

- If you tend to slice the ball, try to make the toe of the club point to the sky **before** it reaches the centre of your chest. By the time it reaches the centre of your chest, the toe should have gone past vertical.

- Finally, make a continuous series of horizontal baseball swings and as you do, gradually bend at the hips to lower the club towards the ground. As you lower the club into a position that looks more like a golf swing, remember to focus on that feeling of rotating the hands to get the club square (or past square) at impact.

7 - FOLLOW THROUGH DRILL

7.1 PROPER FOLLOW THROUGH

- Take your 6 and 7 irons – hold them together, making the best possible grip that you can to ensure that you don't let go of them.

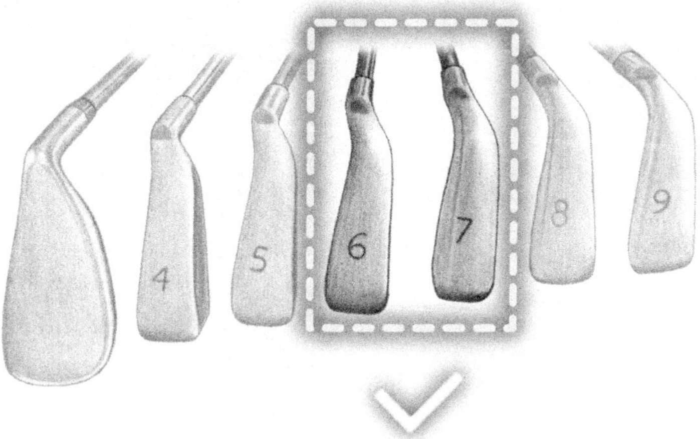

- Hover the clubs away from the ground to ensure that they don't hit the ground or bang together. Swing the clubs gently to start with but also try to make a full and normal follow through.

- The weight of the clubs will pull your body around to a correct and hopefully balanced follow through position.

8 - ANTI-SHANK DRILLS

8.1 AIM TO HIT ON THE TOE OF THE CLUBFACE

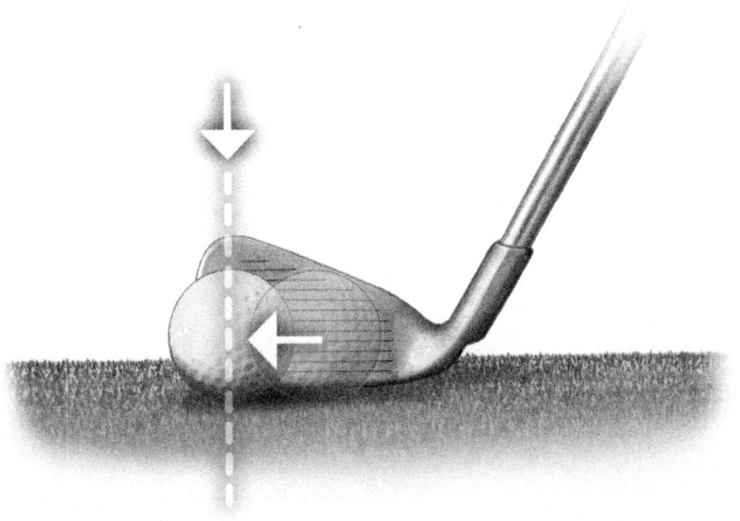

To fix a golf shank so that it never embarrasses you on the course again, we'll quickly recap the causes of shank shots and then look at two drills to eradicate them from your game.

A shank is caused when the ball is struck out of the heel or hosel of the club (see next illustration). What causes that to happen is one, or a combination, of the following:

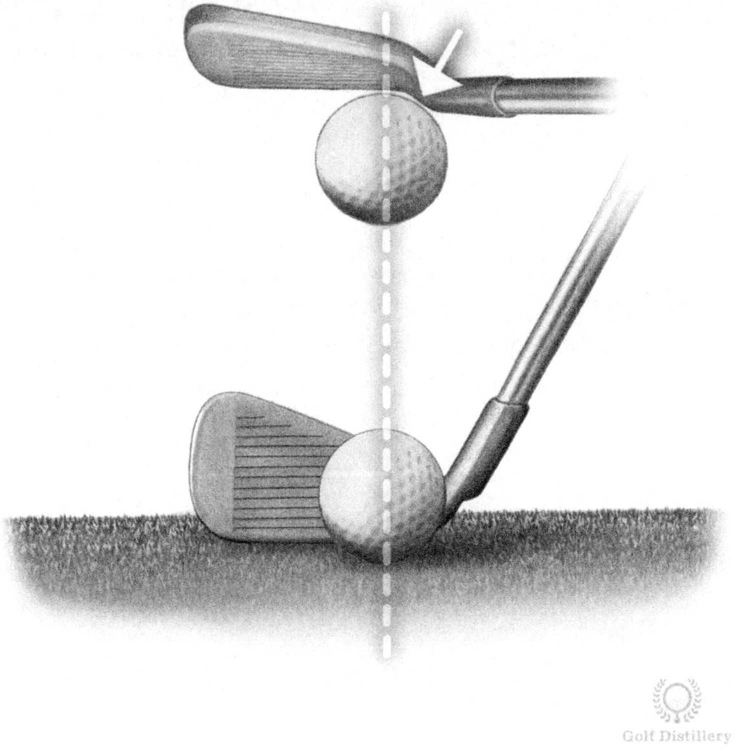

- Setting up too close to the ball
- Poor balance and posture that causes you to fall forwards during the downswing
- An over-the-top (also known as out-to-in) swing path

If you shank the ball on a regular basis, there's a good chance you also suffer from a slice (also caused by an over-the-top swing path).

Assuming you're setting up correctly and have good posture, this drill will all but eliminate shanks from your golf game.

- Using your 7-iron, set up to the ball as normal. Take care to focus on your distance away from the ball as well as maintaining good balance throughout your swing.

- Start by placing the club behind the ball at address and make some good quality practice swings. However, during your downswing, pull the club inwards towards your body so that you actually miss the ball and brush the ground inside the ball. Repeat this process until you can confidently strike the ground in the intended area.

- Now make some swings with a similar feel but this time aim to just clip the ball from the toe edge of the club. Done correctly, this will produce a weak ball flight that shoots out to the right and also sounds like a poor contact. It may even look like a shank but will feel very different.

- Adjust slightly to hit the ball from the middle of the club.

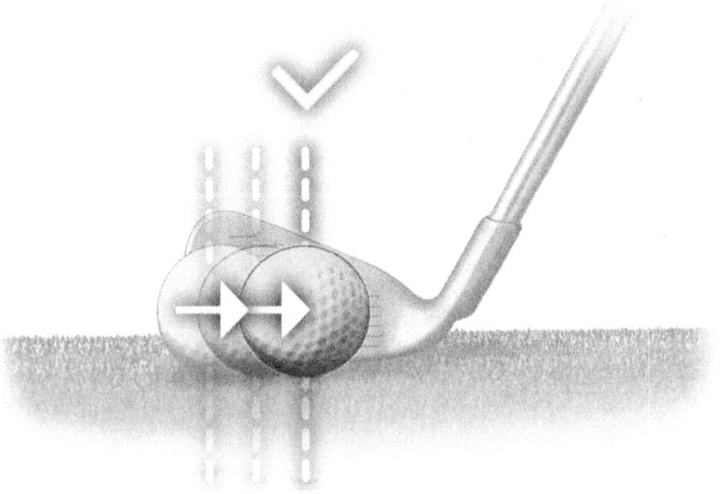

- If ever you're worried about hitting a shank on the course, just make some practice swings addressing a specific patch of ground and then brushing the turf inside that patch by pulling the club in during your downswing. Then set up to the ball and maintain a swing thought of hitting the ball right out the centre of the club.

8.2 HIT THE INSIDE BALL

This golf shank drill is a progression from the previous drill.

It will help you to deliver the golf club on a more in-to-out swing path into the ball. The opposite of this (an out-to-in or over-the-top swing path) is a major cause of shank shots.

Indeed, golfers that shank the ball often suffer from a slice, because this is also usually caused by a swing path that is too much from over the top.

I think you'll find this drill to be very effective in purging shanks out of your game completely.

- Using your 7-iron, set up to the ball as normal, then place another ball about one balls width on the outside.

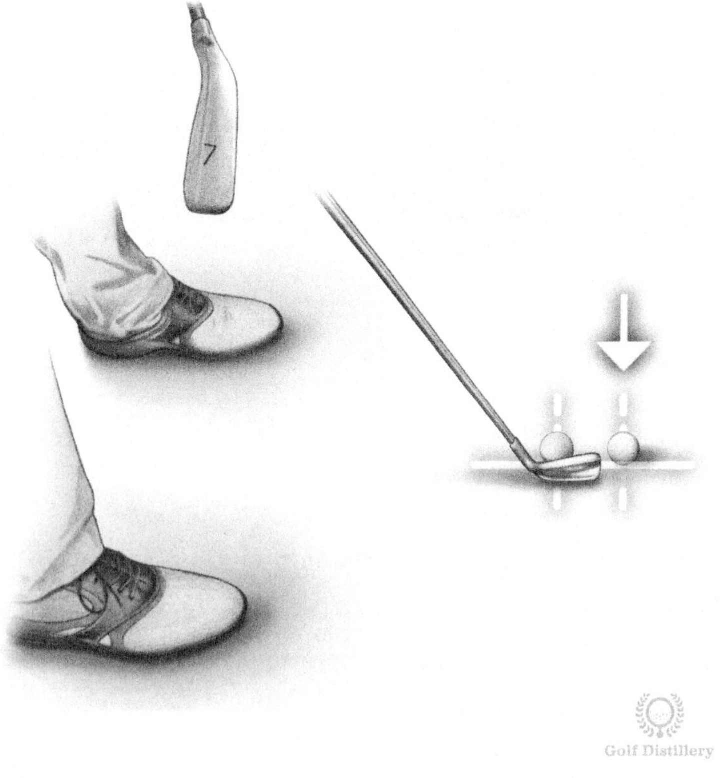

- Now go ahead and address the ball nearest to you (the inside ball). Make a good swing and try to play the inside ball as normal.

- If your swing is correct, the inside ball should fly nicely and the outside ball should remain in the same position. If the outside ball is moved, be aware that your club is not returning to the position at which it was when you addressed the ball.

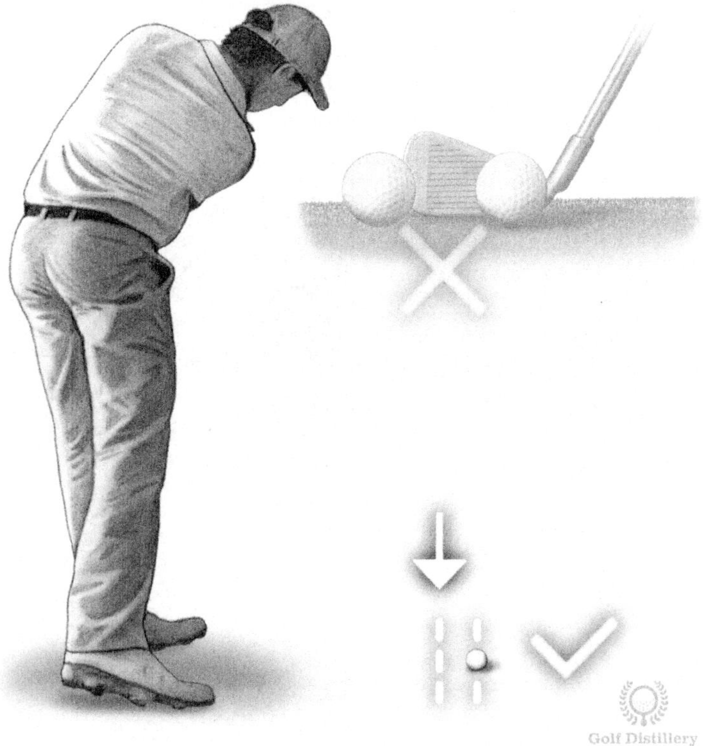

9 - ANTI-SLICE DRILLS

9.1 BASKET GATE DRILL

This first anti-slice golf drill is one of my favourites, simply because I've seen how effective it is with my day-to-day students. It will teach you to deliver the club on an inside or in-to-out swing path – which is the first part of the curing-a-slice equation.

This drill should form the cornerstone of your practice sessions in the immediate future. Try to visit the range 2-3 times a week for the next 2 weeks. Hit 50 balls using the basket setup, really trying to start each ball flight out to the right of the target.

Even if you can't get to the range, you can practice this drill in the yard with an airflow practice ball or even without a ball at all.

- Using a 7-iron, tee the ball up on a small tee peg. Take a couple of driving range buckets (or similar) to use as obstructions.

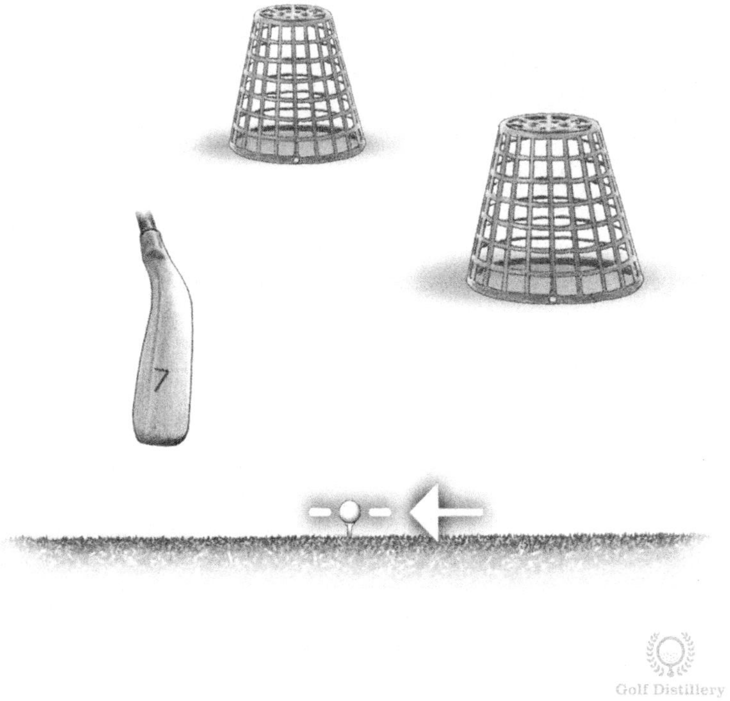

- Place the first basket about 18 inches behind the golf ball. This should allow just enough room for you to make your normal backswing, but it will not allow any room for you to bring the club over the top or on an outside swing path in the downswing.

- Hit between 25 and 50 balls from this position. The ball should block out to the right. Feel how your club is being swung much more from behind your body.

- When you feel comfortable with this drill, take a second basket and place it two feet in front of the ball, but inside the line of the first basket, effectively creating a gate for the club to pass through.

- Hit some balls from the tee peg ensuring you keep the club travelling towards the ball from the inside, but this time also work on extending the club past the second basket. This should create a nice, aggressive in-to-out swing path.

9.2 SPLIT HANDS DRILL

This anti-slice drill will help eliminate slices from your golf game by allowing you to groove a good in-to-out path through the ball.

It's a progression from one of my favourite drills for fixing a slice – the previous one.

- Using a 6 or 7-iron, split your hands up so that your left hand is on the club normally, but your right hand is about 3 inches below the end of the grip.

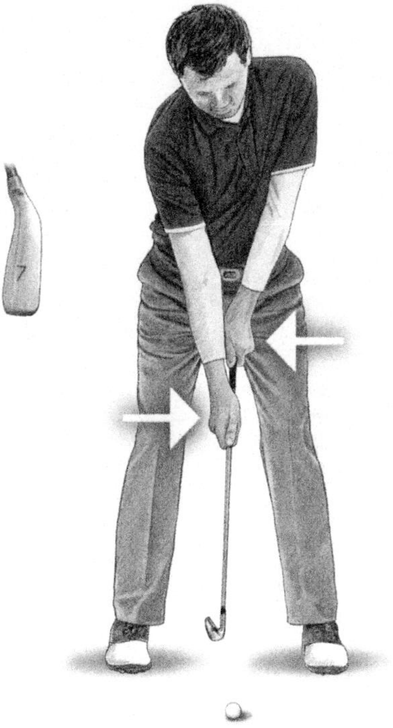

- Make a short backswing. As you change direction into your downswing, focus on dropping the right elbow aggressively into the back of the right hip pocket (for the right-handed golfer).

- This should keep the club behind your body and so promote an inside-outside swing path. Repeat the practice swing a good number of times before trying to feel the same movement but with your hands in their normal grip position.

Once you get the club travelling on a more in-to-out path, it can actually seem like you've made things worse (but it's only temporary)...

A more in-to-out swing path will start the ball out to the right of your target (for the right-handed golfer). Without proper rotation of your hands and forearms, the golf ball will start right and curve further to the right.

So the next step is to work on the proper release of the hands through the ball and the next drill will help you with that.

9.3 BASEBALL SWING DRILL

This golf drill helps you to eliminate slice shots by promoting proper release of the hands through the ball.

If you want to completely eradicate slice shots from your game, you also need to check that your swing path is on the correct line into the ball.

A good in-to-out swing path, combined with proper release of the hands will get you hitting the golf ball consistently straight, or even with a gentle draw.

- Take your normal setup to the ball, and then stand up straight holding the club out in front of your chest as though you were about to swing a baseball bat.

- Swing the club around your body on a horizontal plane (i.e. keeping the club parallel to the ground). As the club comes back in front of your body to an imaginary impact position, take note of the clubface angle. The clubface should be vertical and the toe of the club should point to the sky.

- However, to cure your slice, try to over-exaggerate the rotation of your hands and apply the rotation earlier in the swing. This should produce a clubface which appears to be closed and aiming downwards.

- Repeat this action 20 times, gradually increasing the speed. Then start to tilt at your hips until you feel the club brushing the ground in a normal golf swing type action – but still with plenty of early rotation.

9.4 THE DRIVER DRILL

If you've followed the rest of the drills in this section, you'll be well on the way to hitting the ball consistently straighter than ever before.

But I think the driver needs a bit of extra attention. Because it's the longest club in the bag, it generates more clubhead speed than your irons and fairway woods.

It's this extra speed that can make it difficult for many golfers to release their hands quickly enough through the ball.

The result? The clubface is still open at impact placing clockwise spin on the golf ball that sends it off into the rough.

The drill (see previous illustration) will help you feel what a correct amount of hand rotation feels like.

10 - ANTI-HOOK DRILLS

10.1 HAND ROTATION DRILL #1

This first anti-hook golf drill will help you to control the rotation of your hands through the ball.

A hook shot usually results from a swing path that is too much from the inside (too much from in-to-out), which starts the ball along way right of the target (for the right-handed golfer). The hands and forearms then rotate over very aggressively to 'save' the shot – curving the ball violently from right to left so that it finishes left of your target.

This drill will help you get a feel for controlling the rotation of your hands. But you also want to ensure that your swing path isn't too much on an in-to-out line – which encourages aggressive hand rotation.

- Taking one of your mid-irons, make some pitching-type practice swings. Feel how your hands don't want to rotate during the follow through phase as much as they would for a full swing.

- Take the club through to hip height on the follow through and make a note of the clubface position. Try to keep the blade of the clubface aiming up to the sky and avoid letting the face roll over.

- At the range you can make quite a few of these practice swings before you hit any golf balls. It will help you to get a feel for holding your hands off from rotating. You can then move on to the next drill.

10.2 HAND ROTATION DRILL #2

A hook in golf is usually caused, in part, by hand and forearm rotation that is too aggressive. This second drill will help you get the right amount of feel and timing with your hands so that you can hit the ball straight, or with a soft draw.

- Set up to a ball as normal and then measure one club length down the target line, and place a ball at the end of this club. Next, place 3 balls alongside about 4-6 inches apart (or the width of a clubhead).

- Start by pitch hitting the ball you're set up to over the furthest ball – this should produce a big block shot out to the right.

- Continue hitting pitch shots over the furthest golf ball until you feel you are competent at this block shot. Now increase the power and start aiming your shots over the second ball from the right.

- Again when you feel competent, repeat the process with the next ball and then the next ball.

- Each time increase the power and gradually increase the amount of forearm rotation. You should feel that you gain a valuable education over how much you need to rotate your hands and when they should rotate in order to control your hooking tendencies.

11 - ANTI-THIN SHOT DRILL

11.1 THE BEST BALL STRIKING DRILL

Topped shots in golf are often caused by lifting your chest during the backswing / downswing or by bending the arms through the impact position.

But if you feel that neither of those faults appear in your swing and you're still topping the ball on a regular basis, this drill will definitely help.

In fact, in my experience, when you master this drill you'll cut topped shots (and fat shots) out of your game almost completely. It's an excellent exercise to get you hitting the bottom of the ball, creating a clean, crisp strike every time.

But before, a quick word about taking divots...

A lot of golfers that hit topped or thin shots also hit the ball fat, i.e. the club strikes the ground before the ball causing a very poor contact. Many of their thinned or topped shots are the result of not trying to hit the ball fat.

But striking the turf is an important part of hitting a crisp golf shot... with the aim obviously being to hit the ground after the ball (referred to as 'ball-then-turf').

When you learn to consistently strike the ground after the ball – what that feels like, how your weight shifts to make that happen – it's impossible to either hit the ball fat or top it.

And that's what the following drill will help you achieve.

One of my students, Phil, noticed that before this drill he always tried to 'clip' the ball off the ground (as though the club could only make contact with the turf at that tiny spot right under the ball). Now he is able to take a healthy divot without fear of hitting behind the ball or topping it.

- Place a ball one inch in front of your front foot; it may help if you tee the ball up to start with. Having the ball further forward than you would normally place it with your driver may initially feel very awkward, but stick with it.

- Now go ahead and sweep the ball off the tee and into the air with a nice smooth swing. Really focus on your bodyweight and how it should move aggressively to the left in your downswing.

- Shifting your hips to the left before impact will mean that when the club strikes the ground it will no longer be behind the ball. This should start to give you more confidence that striking the ground and taking a divot is a very positive part of hitting great golf shots.

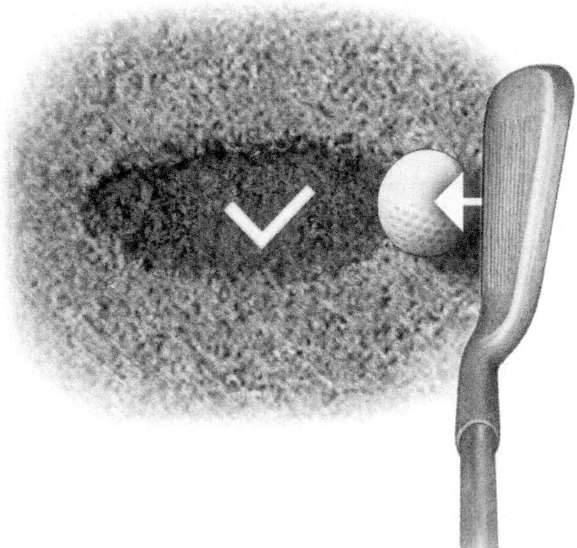

12 - ANTI-FAT SHOT DRILLS

12.1 DIVOT LOCATION DRILL

We've all been there...

You've hit a good drive into the middle of the fairway. The ball is sitting nicely on a lush piece of turf and in your mind's eye you can easily picture the ball cutting through the air and landing softly on a green that is begging to be hit.

And then you hit a fat shot!

The ball travels all of 20 yards – often less than the divot you took along with it!

Fat shots are frustrating and can knock your confidence. The fat shot drills in this section will help you to eradicate fat or heavy shots from your golf game for good.

Not all fat shots are as obvious as taking a huge chunk of turf a good 6 inches before the ball. In fact, you might be hitting the ball a bit fat or heavy on a regular basis without even knowing it (a lot of amateur players do). If this is the case you're losing both power and control over the ball flight.

This first anti-fat shot drill is more of an exercise to help you identify **where** exactly you are taking a divot.

Don't be afraid to take a divot – it's part of creating a solid, powerful strike. However, the divot you take must be after the golf ball – not in front and not even directly beneath it – but immediately after where the ball is resting.

Try it next time you're at the range. Notice where you take the majority of your divots (if you take them at all).

The first step is to make a conscious effort to take a divot immediately after the ball with each swing. You don't even need to hit golf balls to do this. As illustrated previously, simply place a tee peg in the ground, just outside the line of the club's path, opposite to where the front edge of the ball would be.

Once you have completed this drill, continue on to the next fat shots drill.

12.2 FEET TOGETHER DRILL

Note that this anti-fat shot drill requires quite an advanced technique that might feel a bit awkward at first. However, with a bit of practice you'll quickly improve and it will give you a lot of confidence when you come to strike the ball on the golf course.

This drill is great for getting a feel for proper and complete weight transfer.

Don't be put off by how difficult it might seem – it doesn't take a lot of practice to master the sequence and even though you won't hit the ball perfectly every time at first, once you're confident with this drill it will do wonders for your confidence over standard golf shots.

- Use a short iron and tee the ball up on a small tee peg.

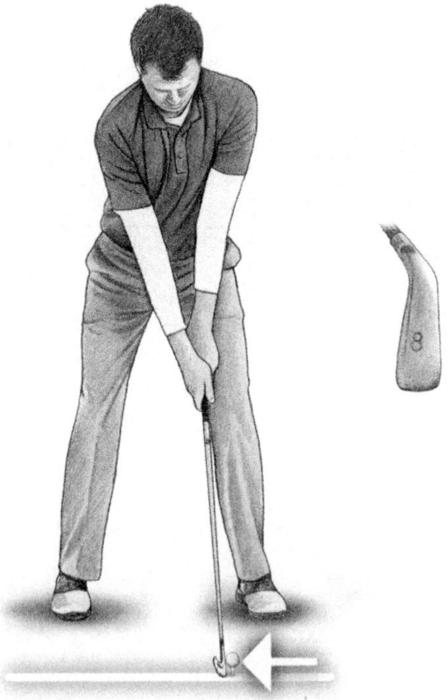

- Start by taking your normal setup. As you swing back slowly, allow your left foot to come completely off the ground and bring it next to your right foot, so that both feet are together.

- At the top of your backswing, as you move into the downswing, shift your left foot back across and plant it on the ground in its original position.

- Accompany this move with a big drive from the hips and a nice, committed weight shift into the newly planted left foot.

- This is a difficult drill to master at first, but when you do you'll be the best ball striker you know!

YOUTUBE CHANNEL LINK

For more golf tips,
visit our YouTube channel:

Golf Distillery

www.golfdistillery.com

ALSO BY GOLF DISTILLERY

Continue on your quest to better golf with these:

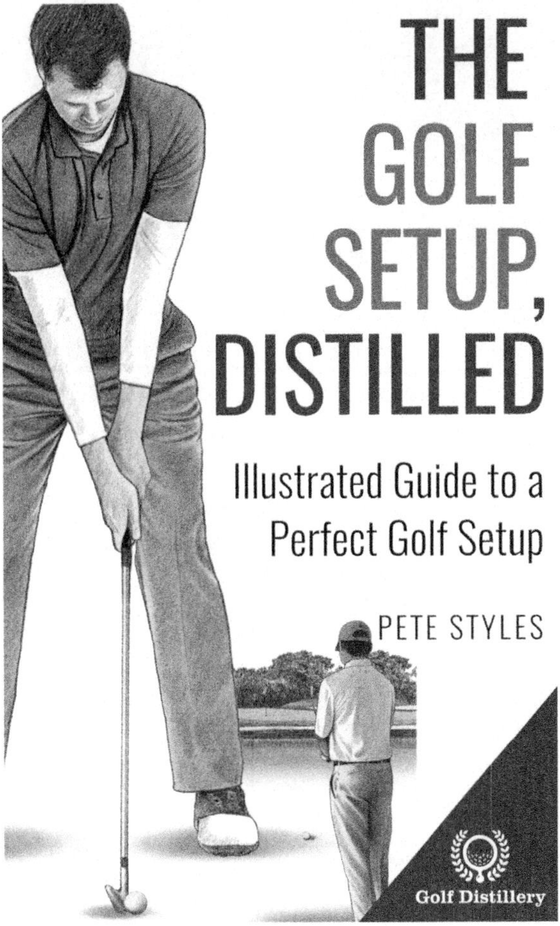

THE GOLF SWING, DISTILLED

Illustrated Guide to a Proper Golf Swing

PETE STYLES

Golf Distillery

6 WEEKS
TO GOLF
FITNESS
How to Get Healthy and Fit, and
Hit the Ball Further Than Ever
PHIL DAVIES
Golf Distillery

PERSONAL NOTES

PERSONAL NOTES

PERSONAL NOTES

Printed in Great Britain
by Amazon

47929129R00096